PIANO • VOCAL • CHORDS

GIGI

LERNER • LOEWE

T0041108

FILM VERSION

Release Date: September 11, 1958

Original Cast Members: Leslie Caron as Gigi, Louis Jourdan as Gaston, Maurice Chevalier as Honoré, and Hermione Gingold as Madame Alvarez

Standout Songs: "Thank Heaven for Little Girls," "I Remember It Well," "The Night They Invented Champagne," "Gigi"

Awards: Winner of nine Oscars®, including Best Picture, Best Director (Vincente Minnelli), and Best Song for "Gigi"

Trivia: Caron's songs were overdubbed by Betty Wand. Audrey Hepburn was slated to play the lead role, but she was filming *Funny Face* at the time, so Caron was selected instead.

STAGE VERSION

Opening Date: November 13, 1973

First Run: 103 performances

Original Cast Members: Karin Wolfe as Gigi, Daniel Massey as Gaston, Maria Karnilova as Mamita, Agnes Moorehead as Aunt Alicia, and Alfred Drake as Honoré

EXCLUSIVELY DISTRIBUTED BY

HAL•LEONARD®

ISBN-10: 0-7390-4987-9
ISBN-13: 978-0-7390-4987-7

GIGI

LERNER • LOEWE

FOREWORD

The story of a teenage girl living in Paris and her relationship with a rich playboy began with the novel, *Gigi*, which was first published by Colette (the pen name for French novelist Sidonie-Gabrielle Colette) in 1945. In 1948, it was adapted for the screen with Danièle Delorme playing the title role. *Gigi* was brought to the American stage in 1951 by playwright Anita Loos, in a production that starred a 22-year-old Audrey Hepburn in her first major Broadway role.

It wasn't until 1958 that *Gigi* was adapted for a film musical version by M-G-M and the team of Alan Jay Lerner and Frederick Loewe, who were, at the time, the toasts of Broadway for their 1956 musical, *My Fair Lady*. The film won nine Academy Awards, including Best Picture, Best Director (Vincente Minnelli) and Best Song (the title song). Today, it is considered the last traditional musical written especially for the screen. Co-star Maurice Chevalier received a special Oscar for his contributions to the world of entertainment. Chevalier's rendition of "Thank Heaven for Little Girls" became a timeless classic. The day after the Oscars, MGM telephone operators answered their phones, "Hello, M-Gigi-M."

An unsuccessful adaptation of the film for Broadway was staged in 1973, starring Karin Wolfe and Alfred Drake.

GIGI

LERNER • LOEWE

CONTENTS

THANK HEAVEN FOR LITTLE GIRLS

Lyrics by
ALAN JAY LERNER

Music by
FREDERICK LOEWE

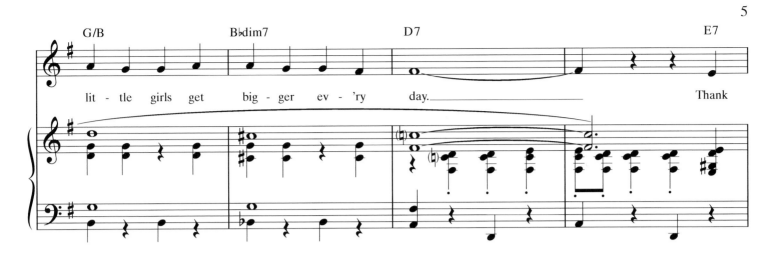

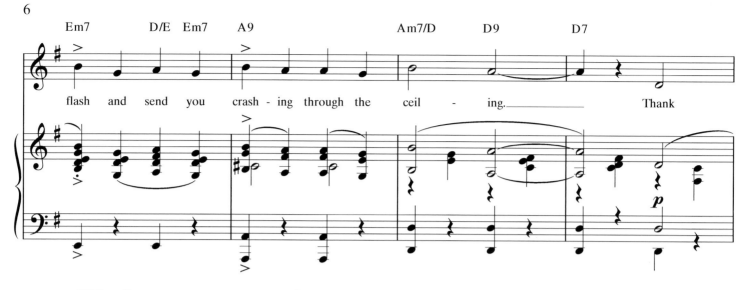

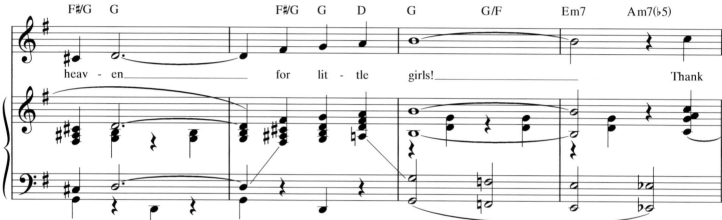

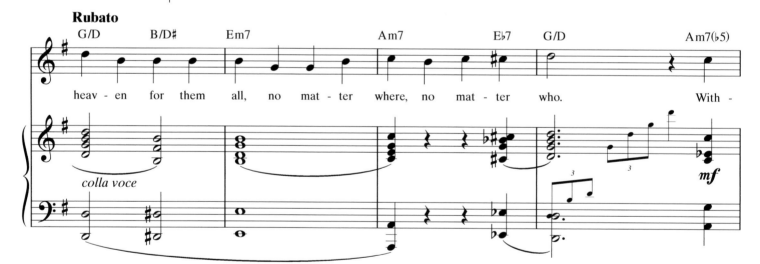

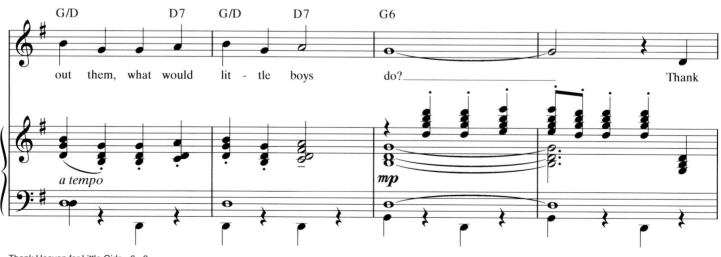

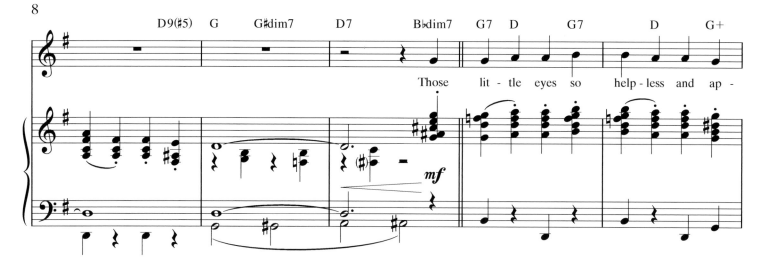

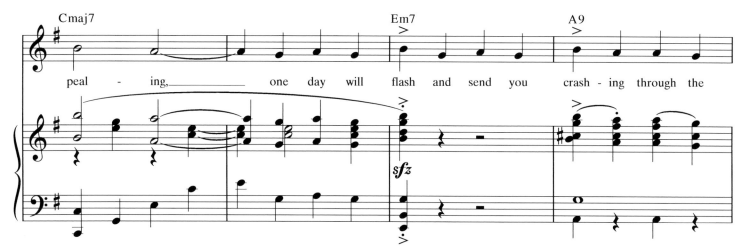

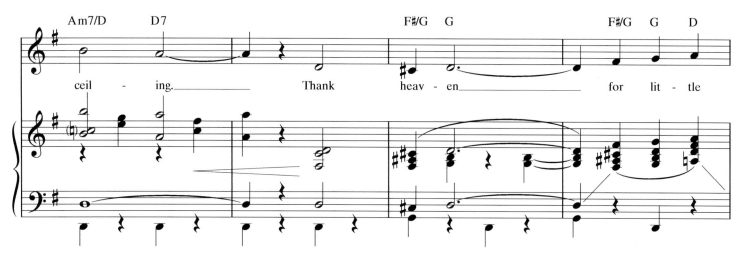

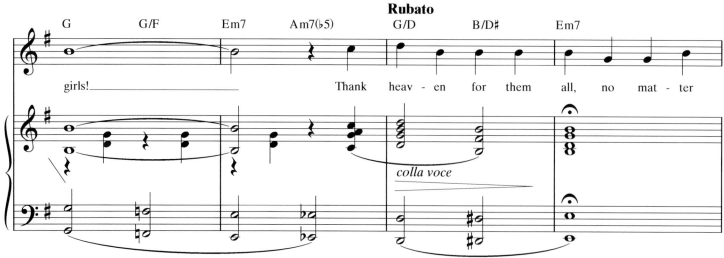

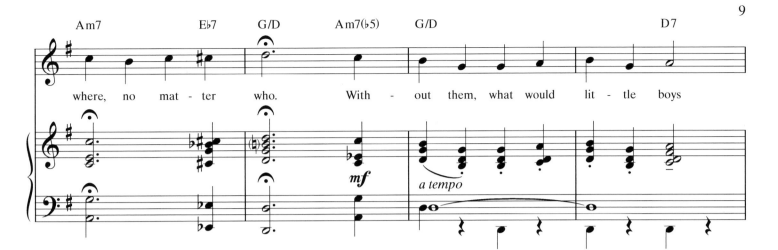

IT'S A BORE

Lyrics by
ALAN JAY LERNER

Music by
FREDERICK LOEWE

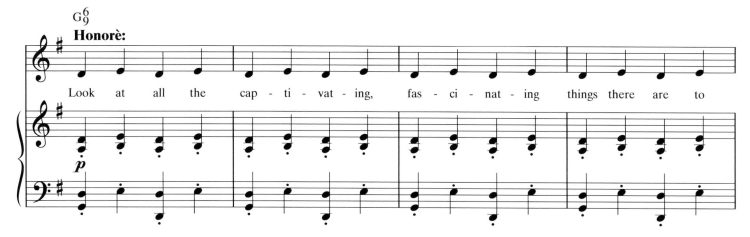

It's a Bore - 8 - 1
29041

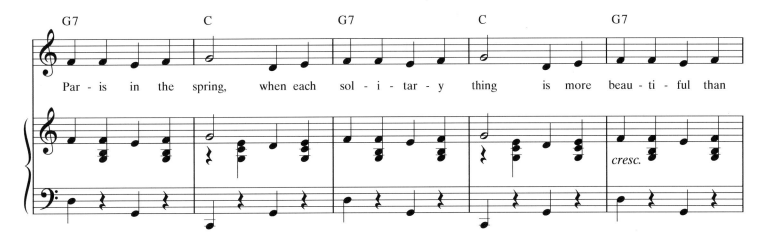

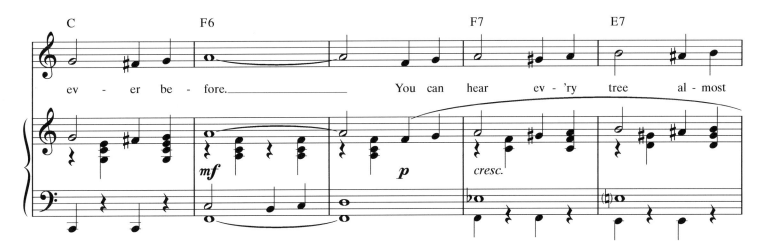

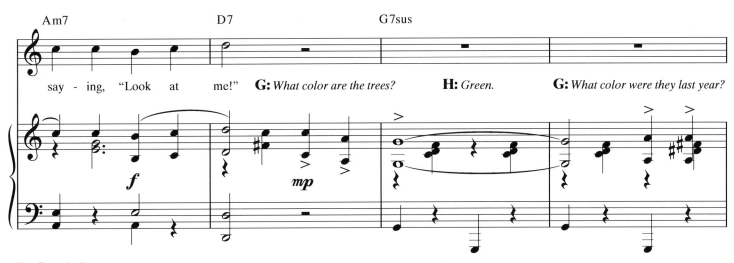

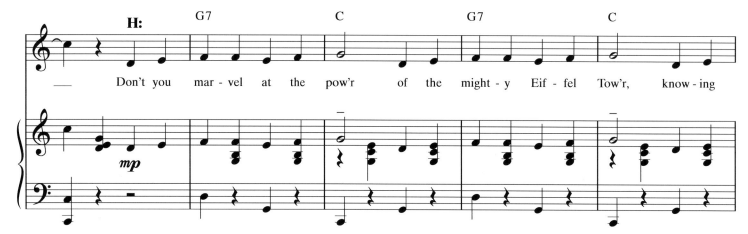

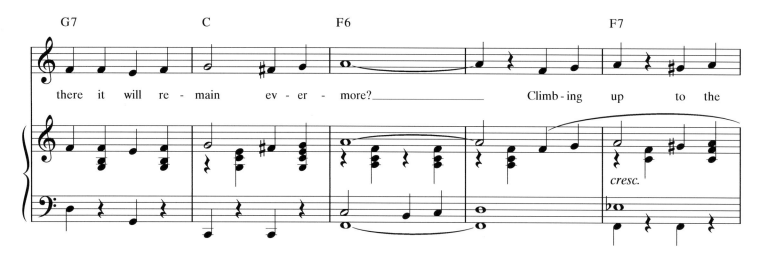

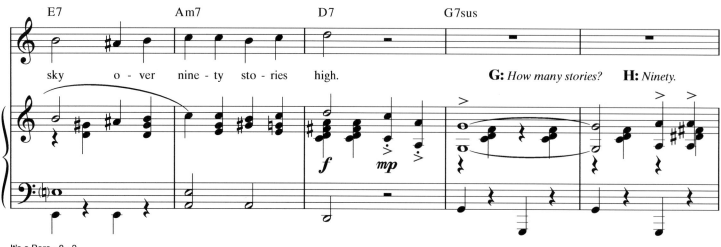

It's a Bore - 8 - 3
29041

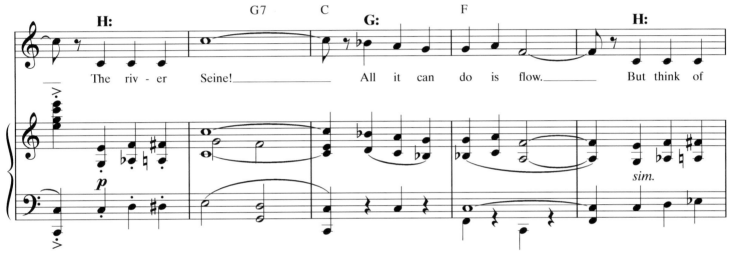

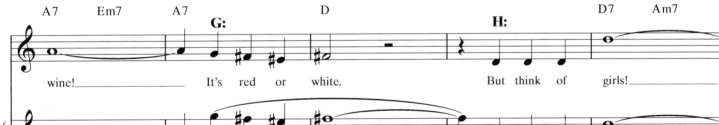

13

G: *How many yesterday?* H: *Ninety.* G: *And tomorrow?* H: *Ninety.* It's a bore.____

H: The riv-er Seine!____ All it can do is flow.____ But think of

wine!____ It's red or white. But think of girls!____

G: It's ei-ther yes or no,____ and if it's no or if it's yes, it sim-ply

It's a Bore - 8 - 4
29041

14

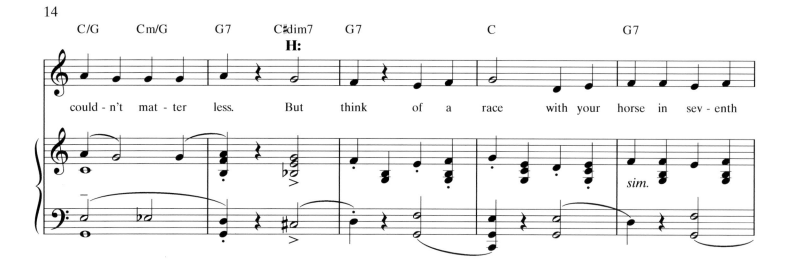

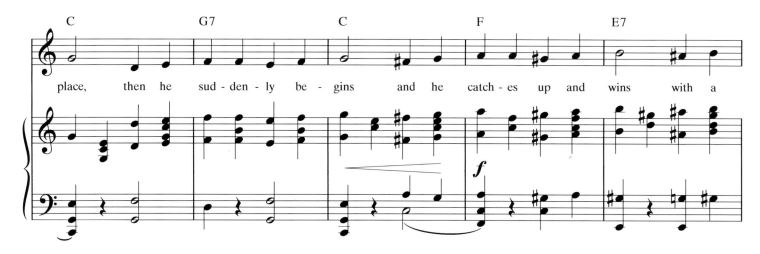

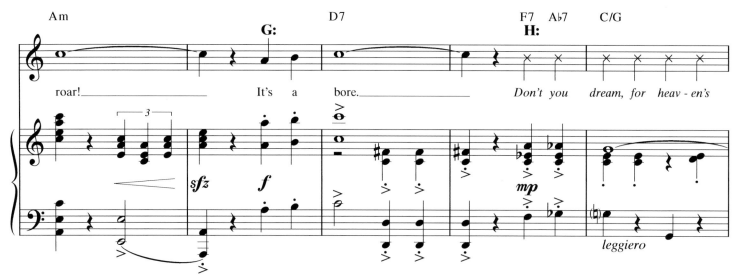

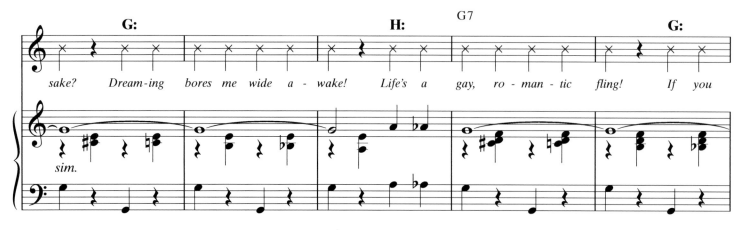

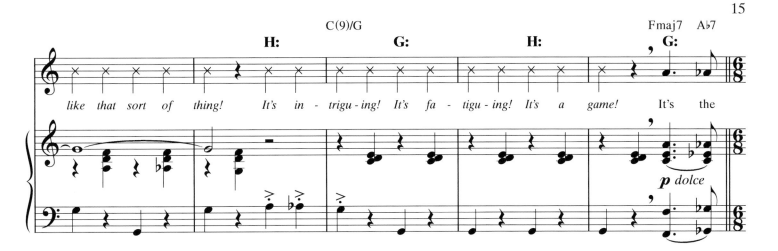

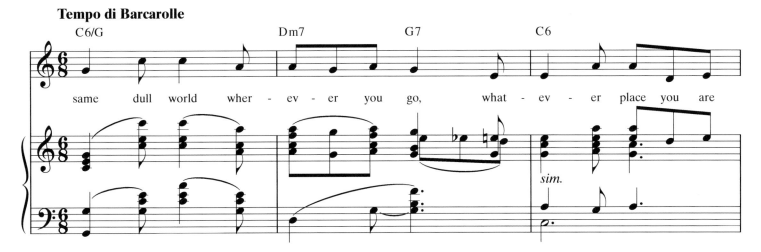

Tempo di Barcarolle

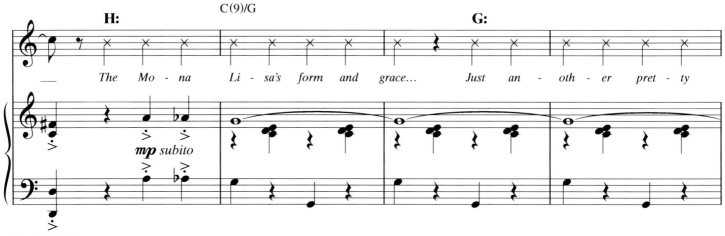

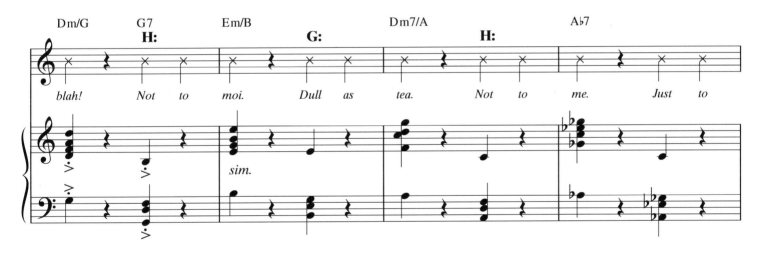

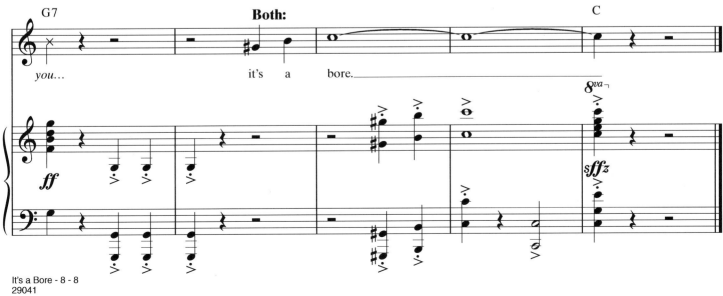

It's a Bore - 8 - 8
29041

THE EARTH AND OTHER MINOR THINGS

Lyrics by
ALAN JAY LERNER

Music by
FREDERICK LOEWE

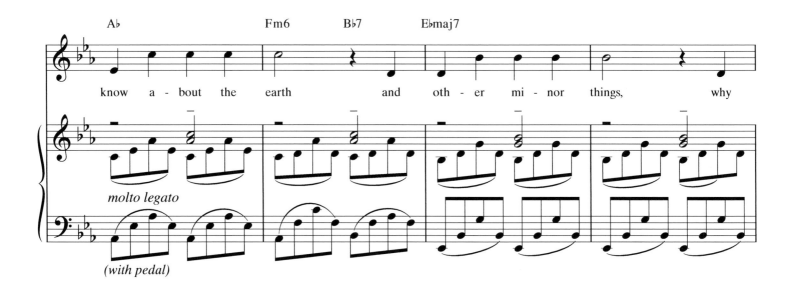

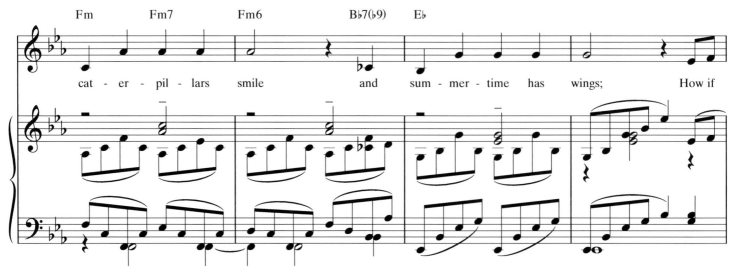

The Earth and Other Minor Things - 4 - 1
29041

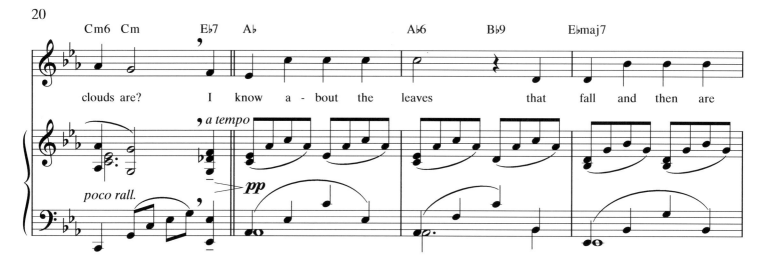

clouds are? I know a - bout the leaves that fall and then are

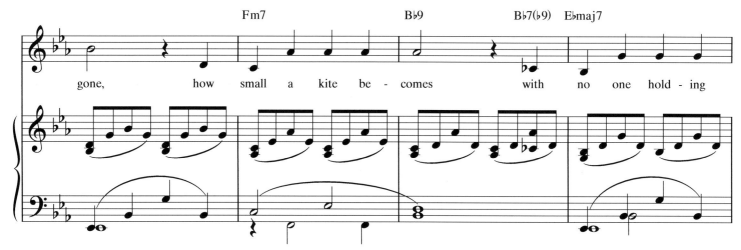

gone, how small a kite be - comes with no one hold - ing

on; and I can't be a cloud in a storm with

no - where to go to be warm; And as long as I can't find a

clue to the rid-dle of it, what am I to do in the mid-dle of it

poco rall.

a tempo

all? I don't be-long where the crowds are.

mp

I don't be-long where the clouds are. Then where do

pp

poco rall.

pp a tempo

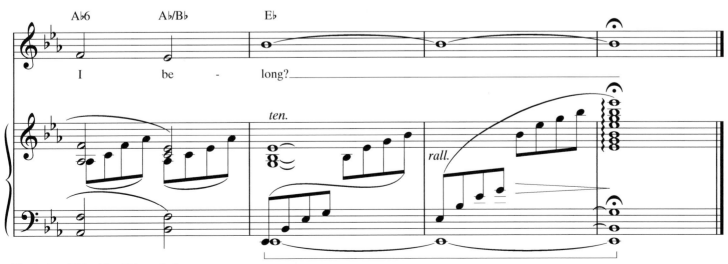

I be - long?

ten.

rall.

PARIS IS PARIS AGAIN

Lyrics by
ALAN JAY LERNER

Music by
FREDERICK LOEWE

park! A shot in the dark! And Par - is is spic - i - ly,

vic - e - ly Par - is a - gain.

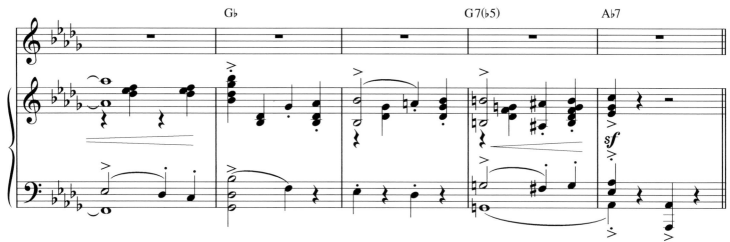

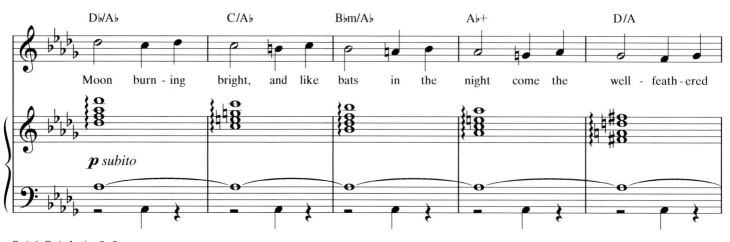

Moon burn - ing bright, and like bats in the night come the well - feath - ered

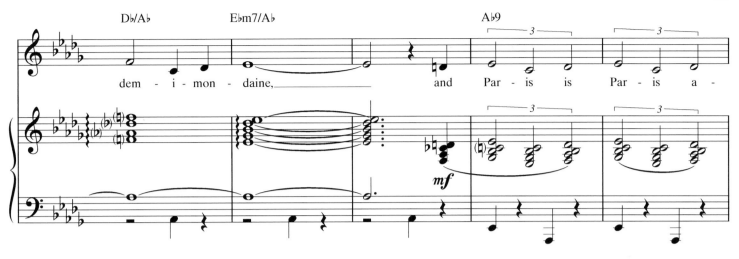

dem - i - mon - daine, _____ and Par - is is Par - is a -

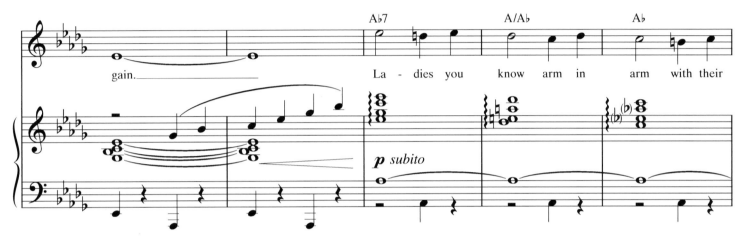

gain. _____ La - dies you know arm in arm with their

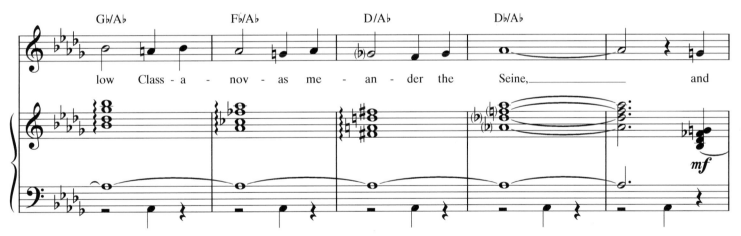

low Class - a - nov - as me - an - der the Seine, _____ and

Par - is is Par - is a - gain. _____ Meet - ings at

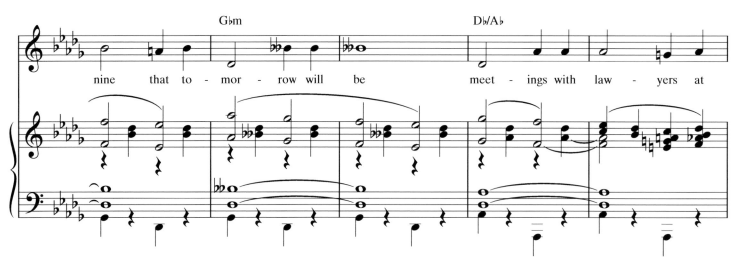

nine that to - mor - row will be   meet - ings with law - yers at

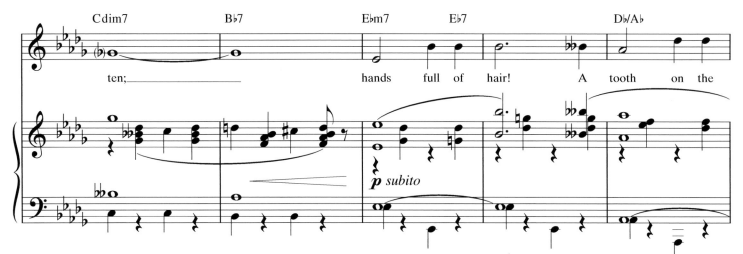

ten;_____   hands full of hair! A tooth on the

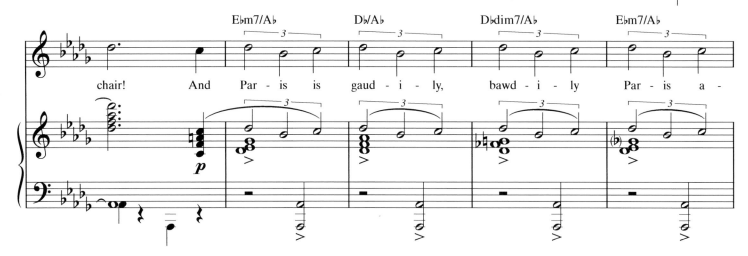

chair! And Par - is is gaud - i - ly, bawd - i - ly Par - is a -

gain._____

SHE IS NOT THINKING OF ME

Lyrics by
ALAN JAY LERNER

Music by
FREDERICK LOEWE

Tempo di valse (moderately)

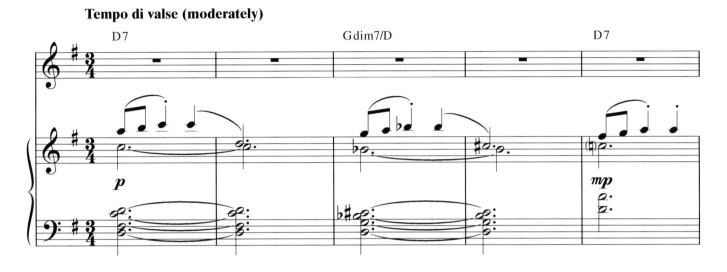

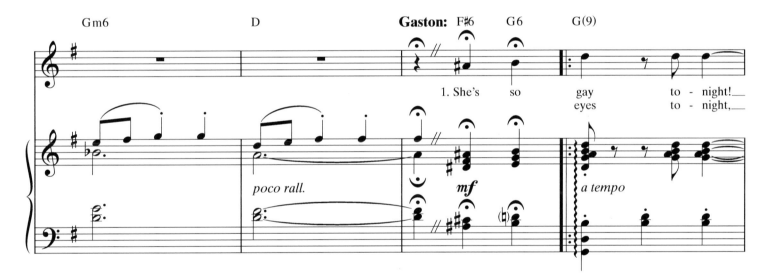

She Is Not Thinking of Me - 11 - 1
29041

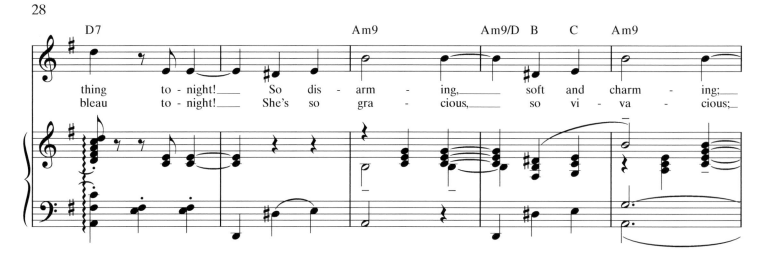

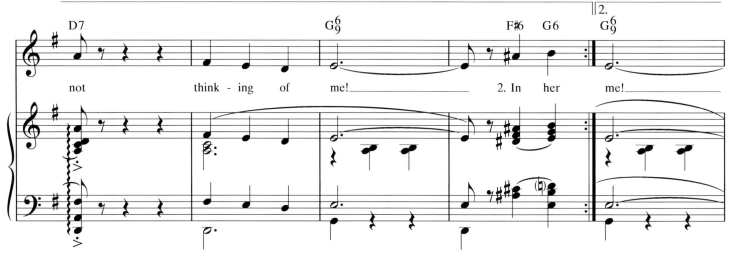

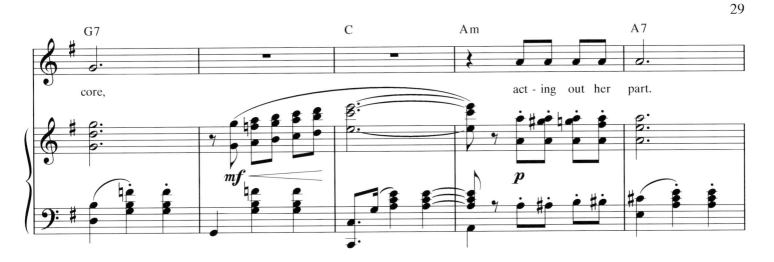

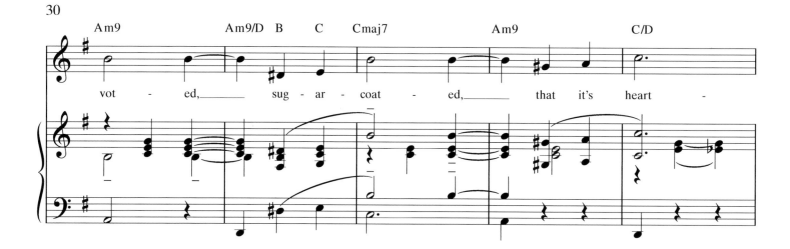

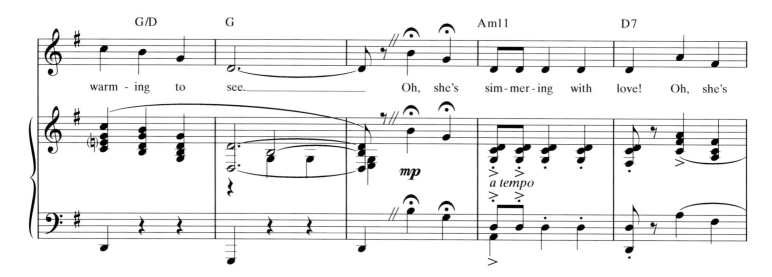

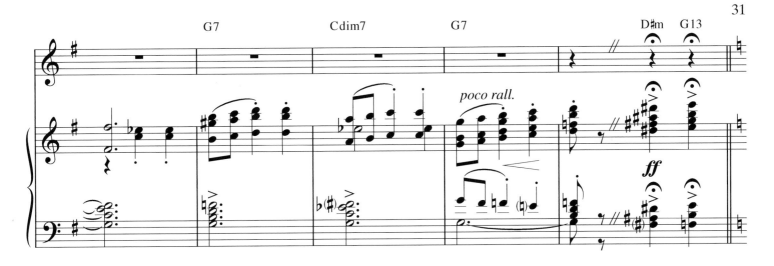

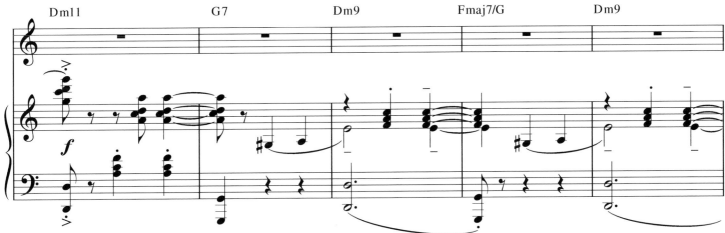

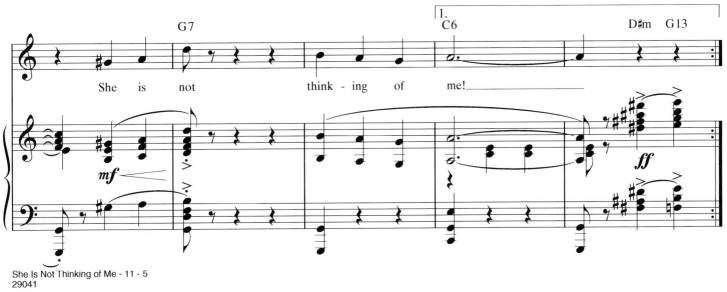

She is not think-ing of me!_____

32

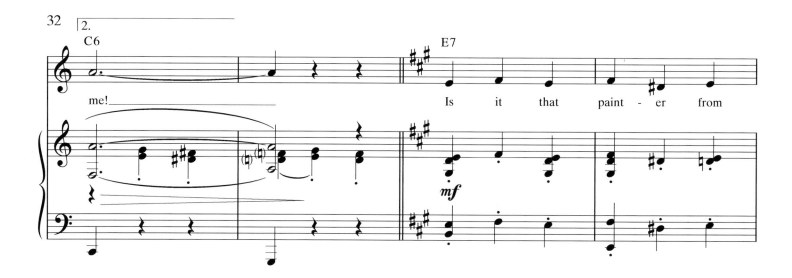

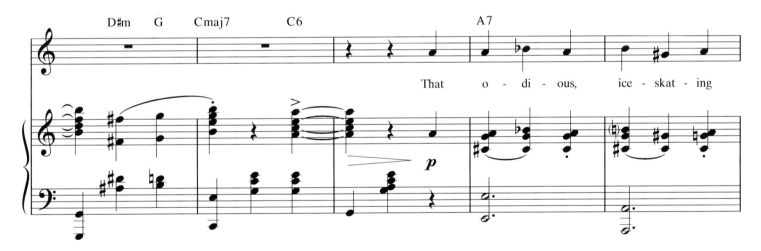

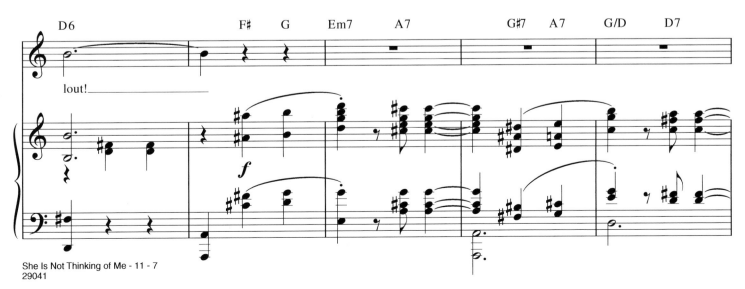

She Is Not Thinking of Me - 11 - 7
29041

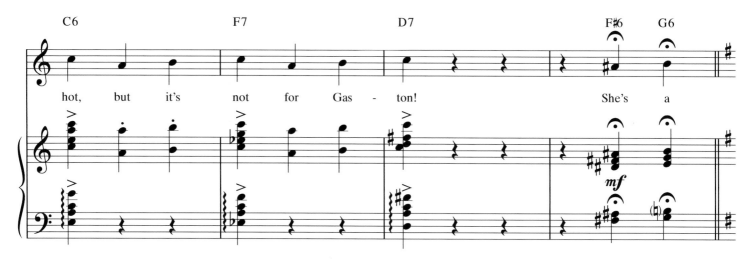

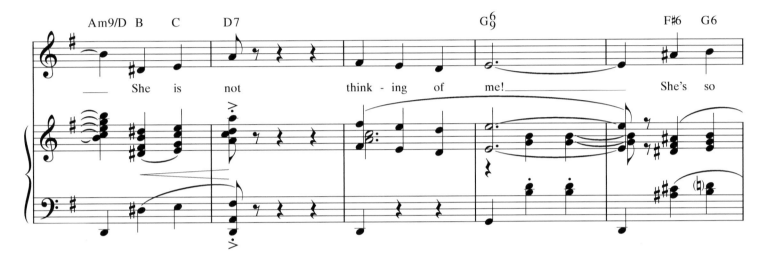

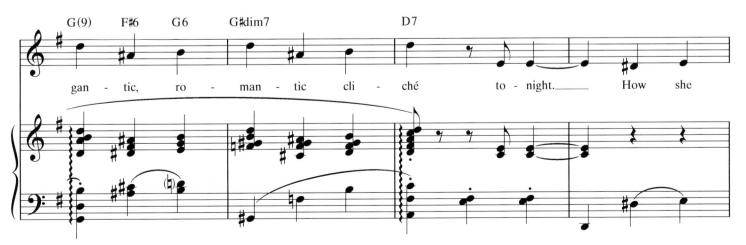

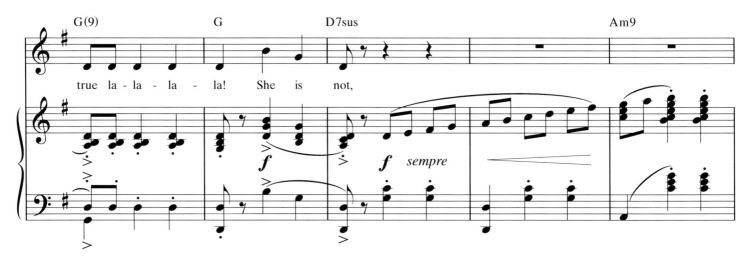

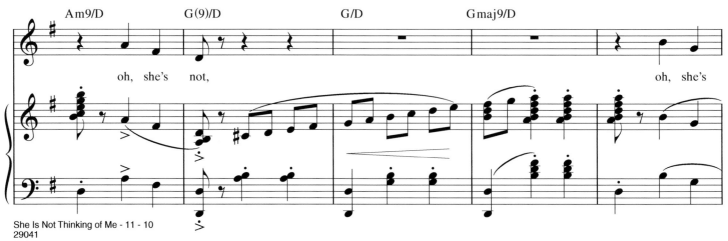

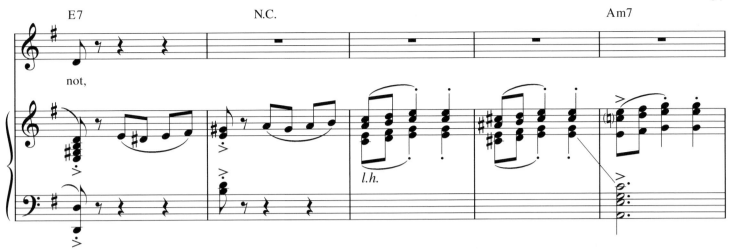

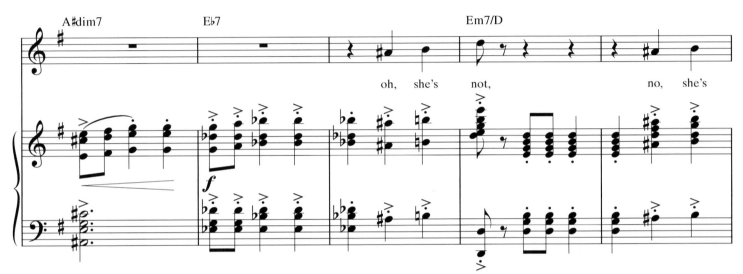

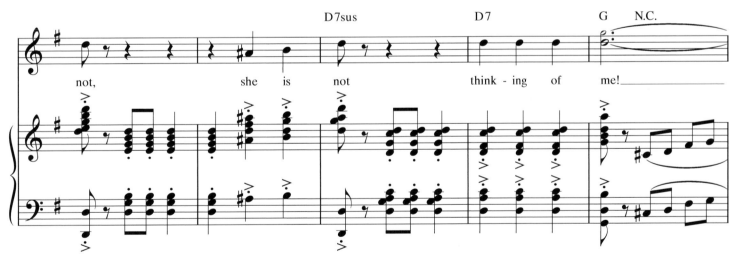

THE NIGHT THEY INVENTED CHAMPAGNE

Lyrics by
ALAN JAY LERNER

Music by
FREDERICK LOEWE

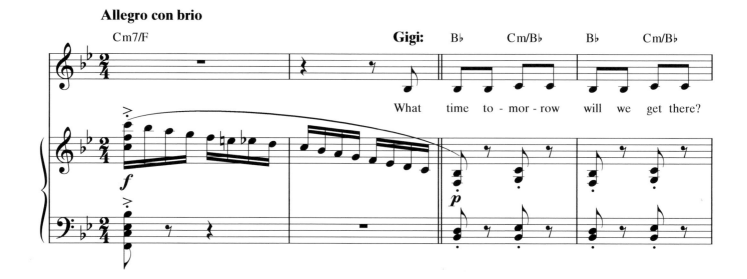

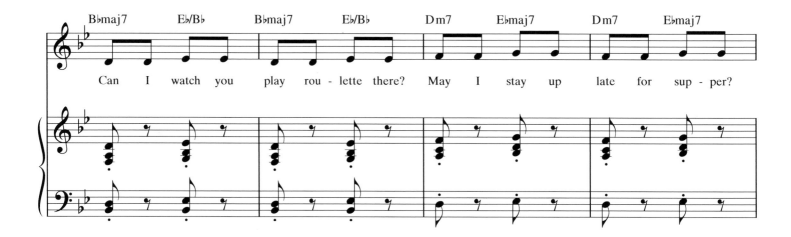

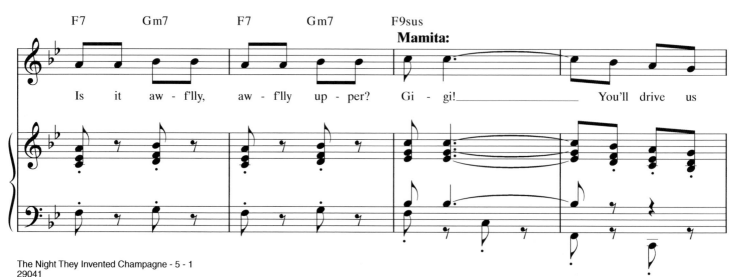

The Night They Invented Champagne - 5 - 1
29041

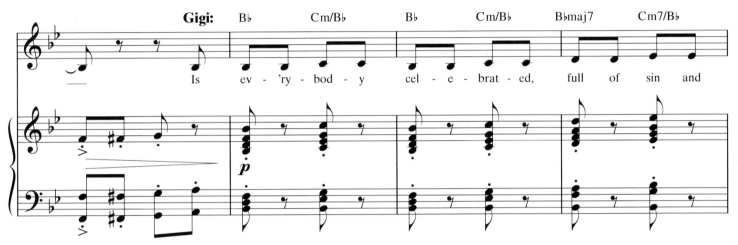

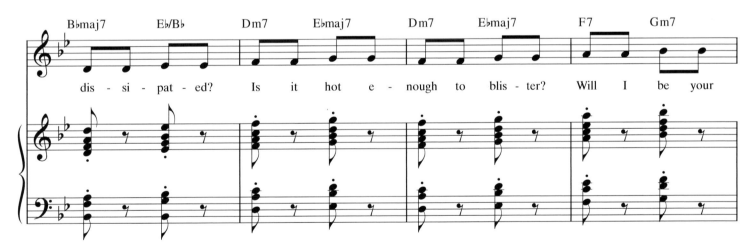

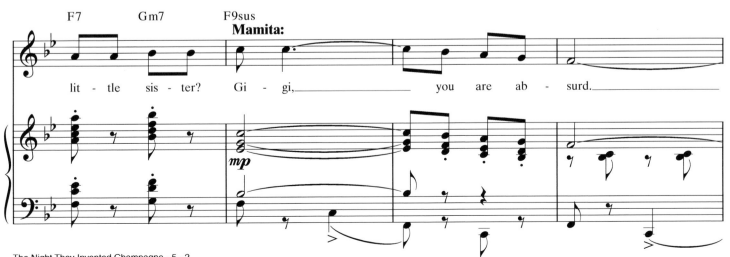

Not an - oth - er word.

Gaston:

Bb

Fsus F Bb

Let her gush and jab - ber. Let her be en - thused. I can - not re -

C7 F7 Cm7 F7 Bb Fm7 Bb7 **Gigi:**

mem - ber when I have been more a - mused. The

Eb

night they in - vent - ed cham - pagne, it's

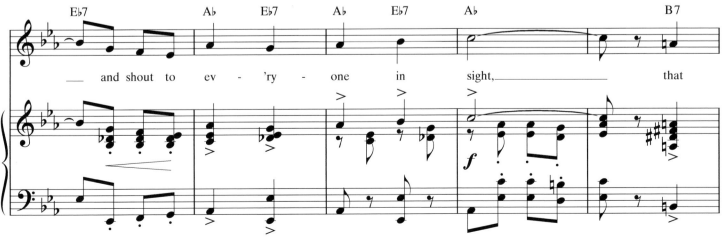

since the world be - gan, no wom - an or a man has ev - er been as

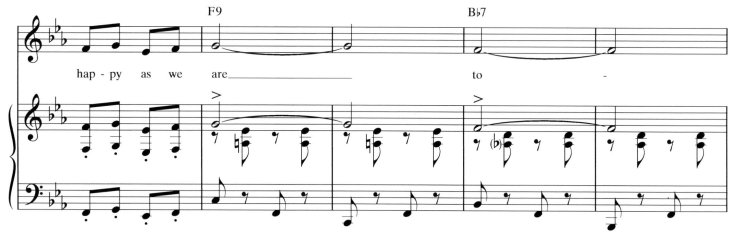

hap - py as we are_____ to -

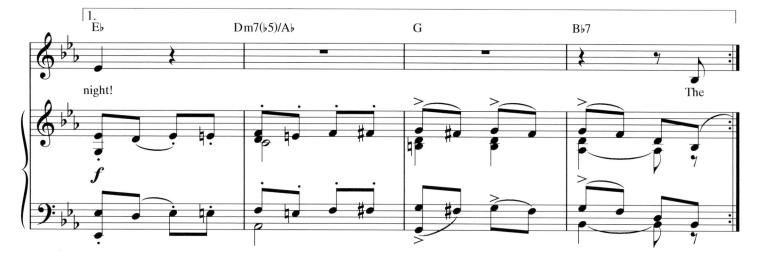

1.

night!   The

2.

night!

SAINT-SUBBER
presents
The Los Angeles and San Francisco Light Opera Production of

Loewe and Lerner's

GiGi

A New Musical for Broadway
based on the novel by Colette

Music by
FREDERICK LOEWE

Book and Lyrics by
ALAN JAY LERNER

Produced by **EDWIN LESTER** and **SAINT-SUBBER**

Scenic Production Designed by **OLIVER SMITH**

Costumes Designed by **OLIVER MESSEL**

Lighting by **THOMAS SKELTON**

Orchestrations by **IRWIN KOSTAL**   Dance Arrangements by **TRUDE RITTMANN**

Musical Direction by **ROSS REIMUELLER**

Dances and Musical Numbers Staged by
ONNA WHITE

Directed by
JOSEPH HARDY

I REMEMBER IT WELL

Lyrics by
ALAN JAY LERNER

Music by
FREDERICK LOEWE

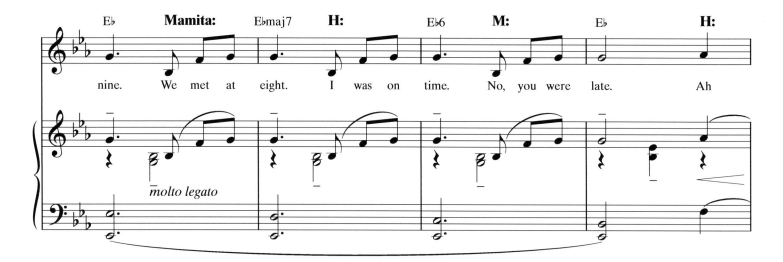

I Remember It Well - 6 - 1
29041

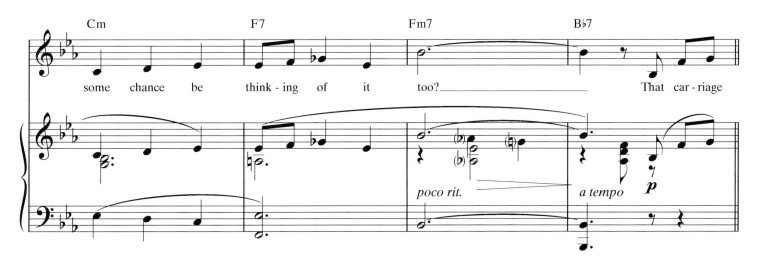

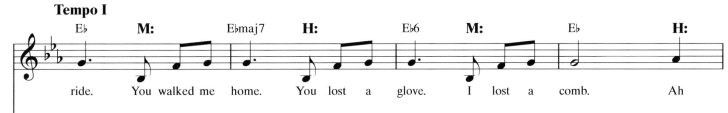

Tempo I

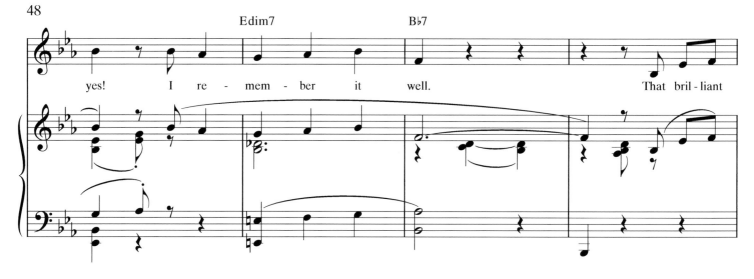

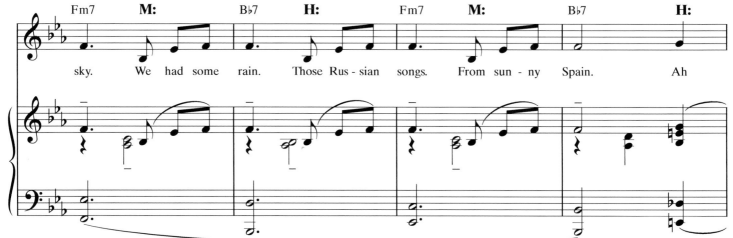

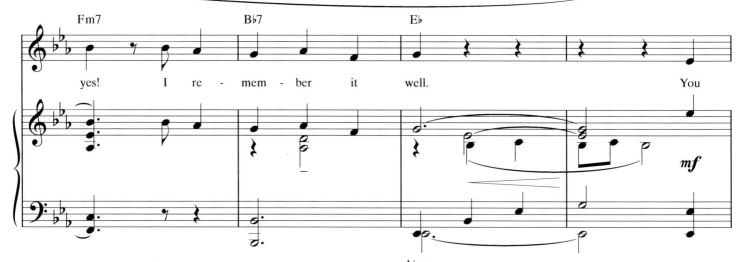

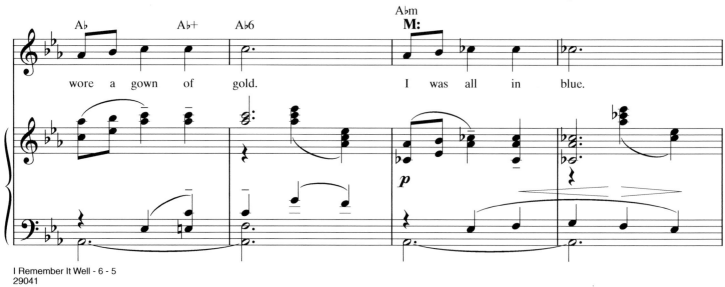

GIGI

Lyrics by
ALAN JAY LERNER

Music by
FREDERICK LOEWE

Gigi - 6 - 1
29041

where, oh where did Gi - gi go?

Moderato, molto espressivo

Refrain

Gi - gi, am I a fool with-out a mind or have I mere - ly been too blind to re - al -

ize? Oh, Gi - gi, why you've been grow - ing up be - fore my

eyes! Gi - gi, you're not at

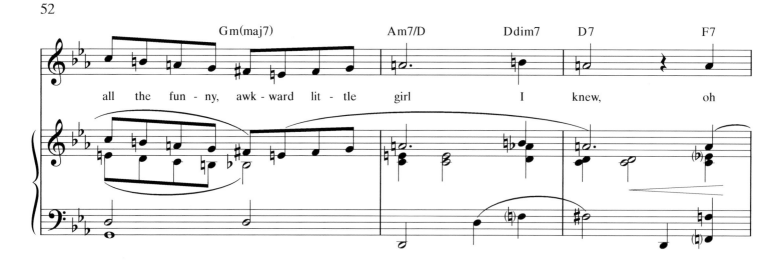

all the fun - ny, awk - ward lit - tle girl I knew, oh

no! O - ver - night there's been a breath - less change in

you. Oh, Gi - gi, while you were trem-bling on the brink, was I out

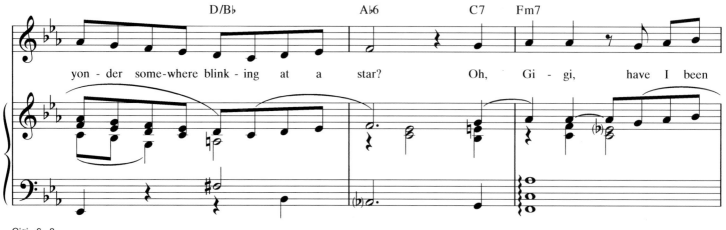

yon - der some-where blink - ing at a star? Oh, Gi - gi, have I been

standing up too close, or back too far?_____ When did your

sparkle turn to fire and your warmth become desire? Oh, what

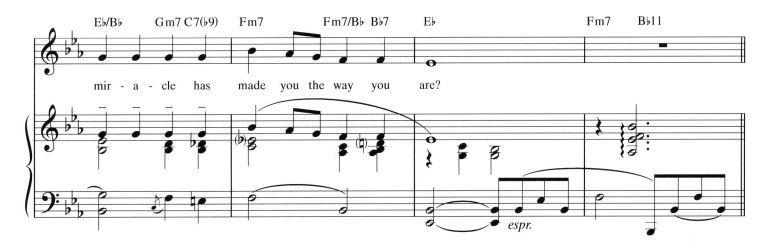

miracle has made you the way you are?

Gigi, am I a fool without a mind or have I merely been too blind to real-

54

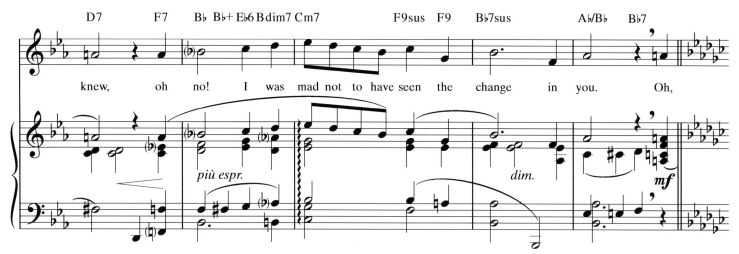

Gigi - 6 - 5
29041

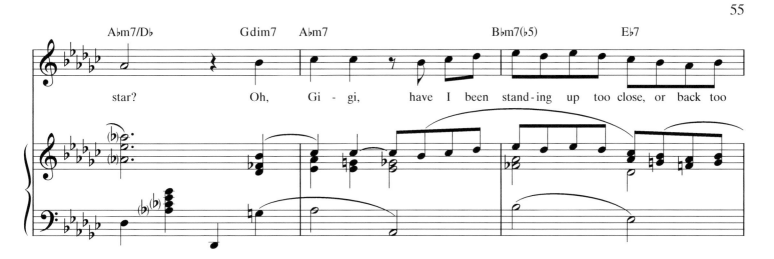

star?   Oh,   Gi - gi,   have   I   been   stand-ing   up   too   close,   or   back   too

far?_____   When   did   your   spar - kle   turn   to

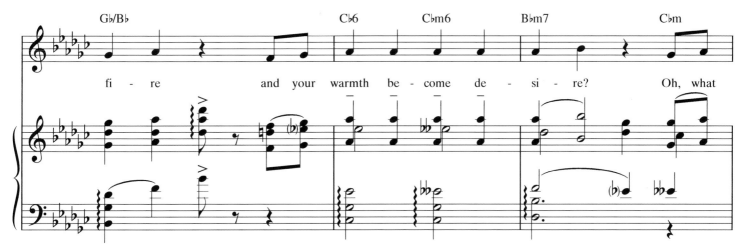

fi - re   and   your   warmth   be - come   de - si - re?   Oh,   what

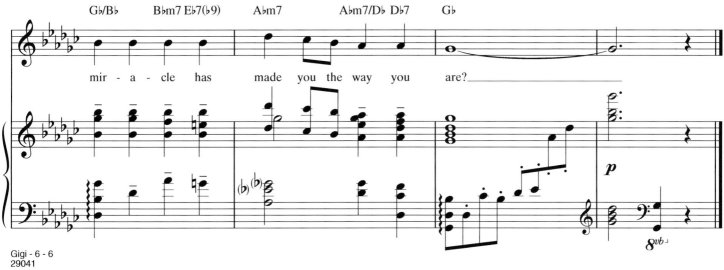

mir - a - cle   has   made   you   the   way   you   are?_____

I'M GLAD I'M NOT YOUNG ANYMORE

Lyrics by
ALAN JAY LERNER

Music by
FREDERICK LOEWE

Poor boy, poor boy, down-heart-ed and de-pressed and in a

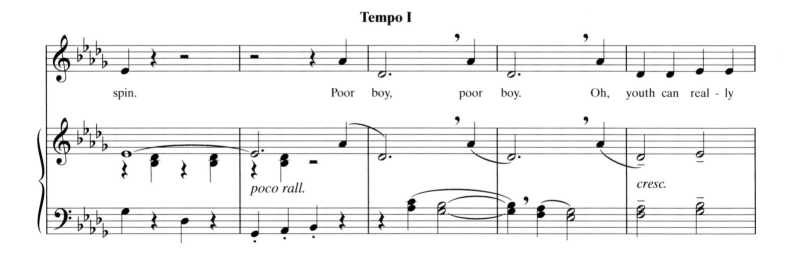

spin. Poor boy, poor boy. Oh, youth can real-ly

do a fel-low in. 1. How

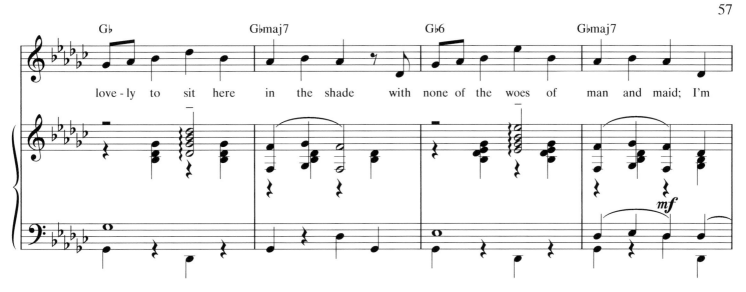

love-ly to sit here in the shade with none of the woes of man and maid; I'm

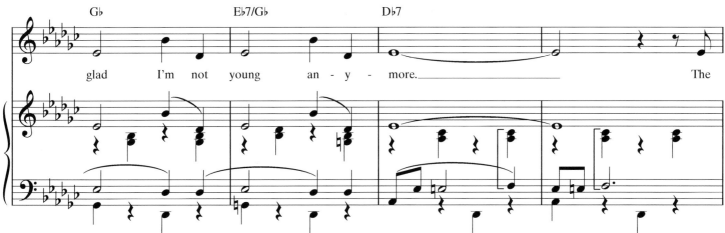

glad I'm not young an - y - more._____ The

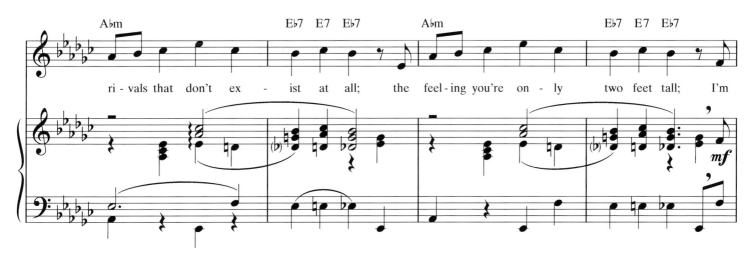

ri - vals that don't ex - ist at all; the feel-ing you're on - ly two feet tall; I'm

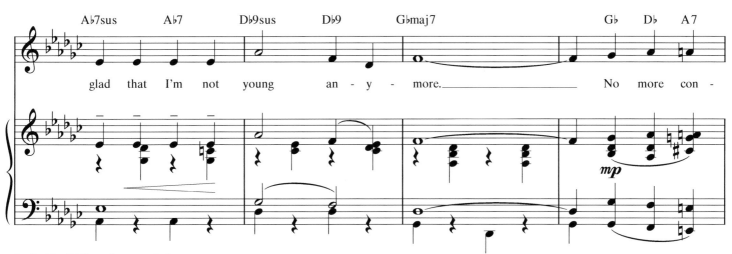

glad that I'm not young an - y - more._____ No more con -

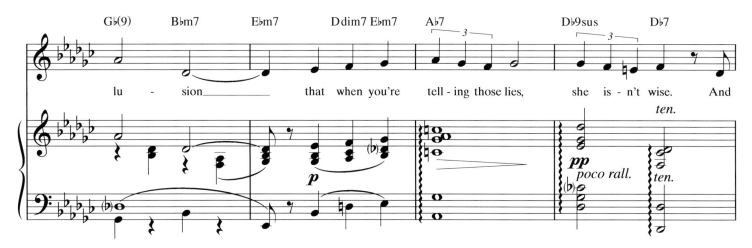

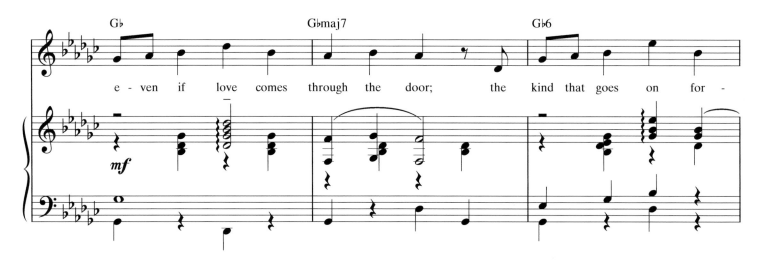

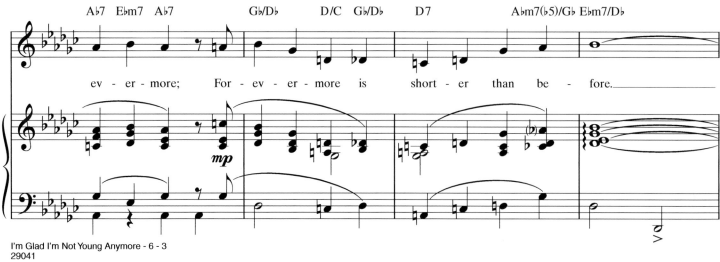

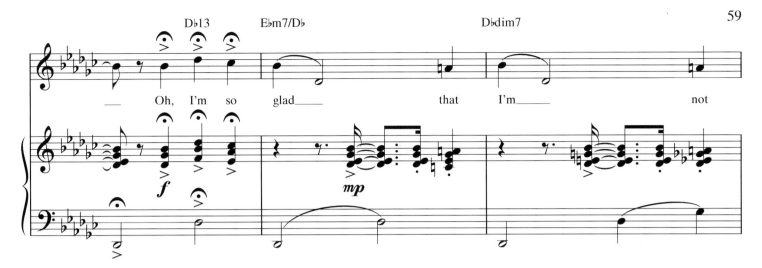

Oh, I'm so glad___ that I'm___ not

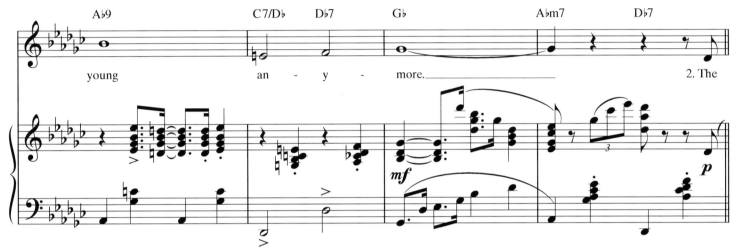

young an - y - more.___ 2. The

ti - ny re - mark that tor - tures you, the fear that your friends won't like her too; I'm

glad I'm not young an - y - more.___ The

long-ing to end a stale af-fair, un-til you find out she does-n't care; I'm

glad that I'm not young an - y - more._____ No more frus -

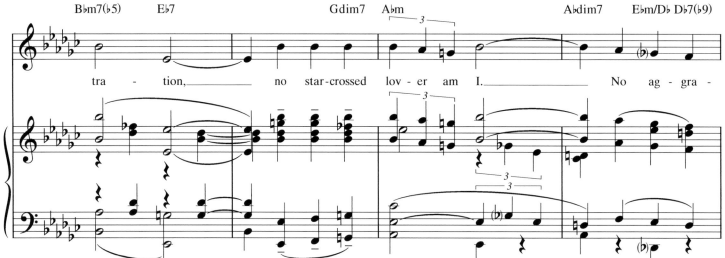

tra - tion,_____ no star-crossed lov-er am I._____ No ag-gra -

va - tion,_____ just one re - luc-tant re - ply, "La - dy, good-bye." The

IN THIS WIDE, WIDE WORLD

Lyrics by
ALAN JAY LERNER

Music by
FREDERICK LOEWE

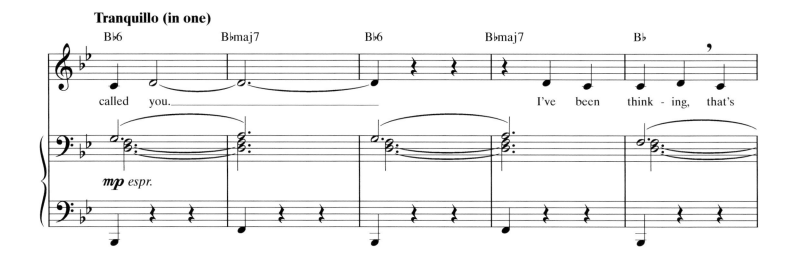

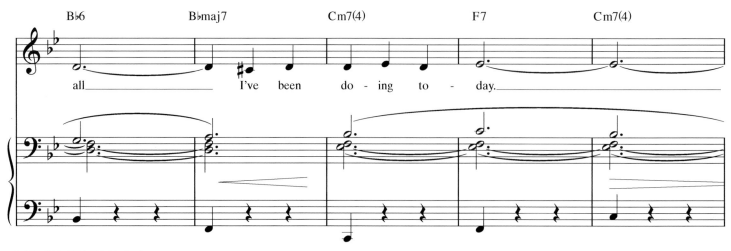

In This Wide, Wide World - 6 - 1
29041

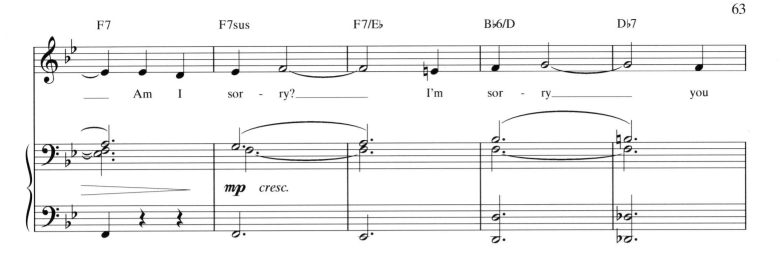

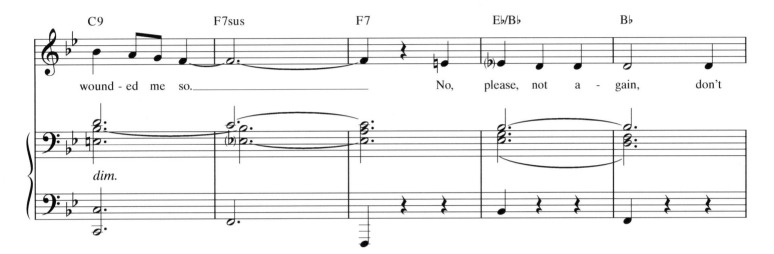

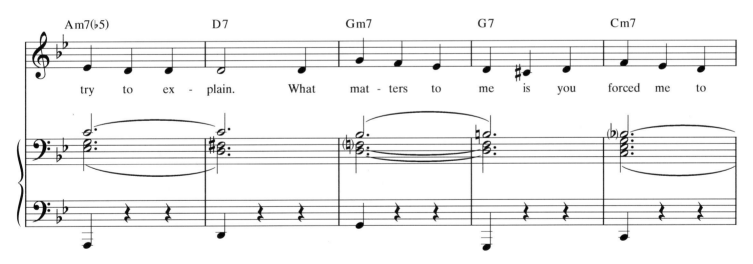

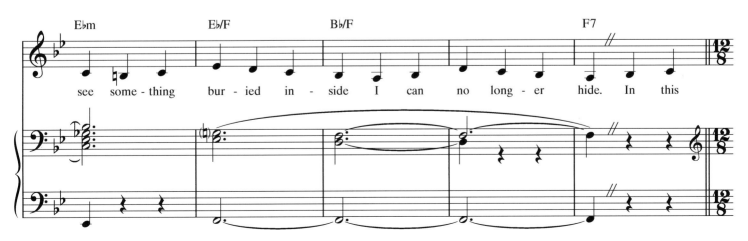

more_____ your world:_____ wis - er

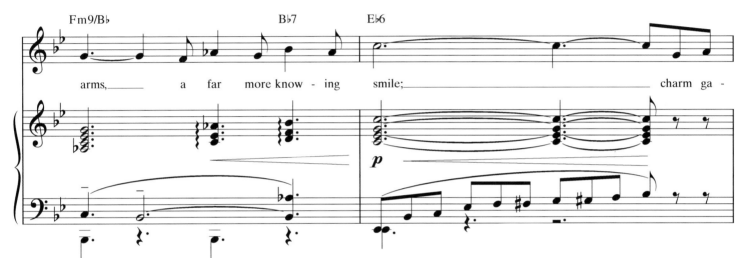

arms,_____ a far more know - ing smile;_____ charm ga -

lore she'll have, much more she'll have than I pos - sess;_____ with so much

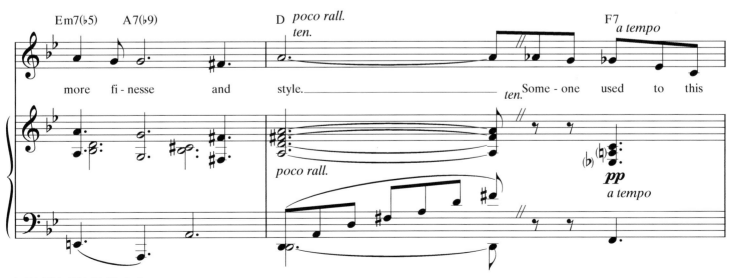

more fi - nesse and style._____ Some - one used to this

wide,_____ wide world,_____ who can

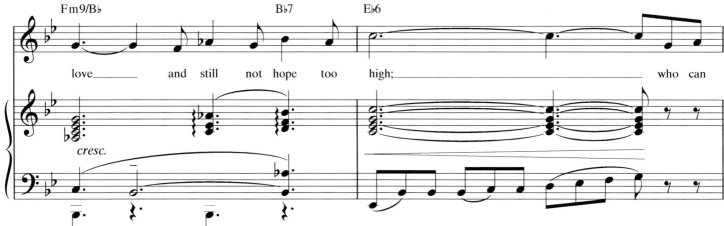

love_____ and still not hope too high;_____ who can

live your life and give your life the things I can't sup - ply! And if you

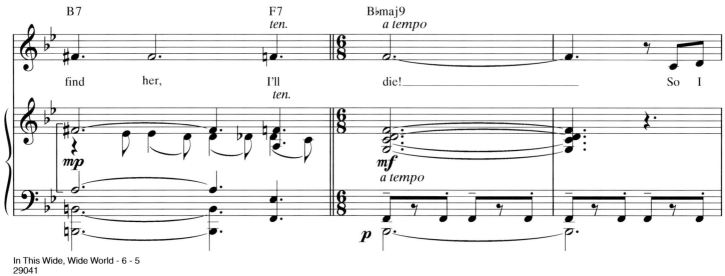

find her, I'll die!_____ So I

LYRICS SECTION

THANK HEAVEN FOR LITTLE GIRLS

Honoré: *(Spoken) And here is the future.*
Someday she will either be married or unmarried.
Mademoiselle…

Each time I see a little girl of five or six or seven,
I can't resist the joyous urge to smile and say…
Thank heaven for little girls!
For little girls get bigger ev'ry day.
Thank heaven for little girls!
They grow up in the most delightful way.
Those little eyes so helpless and appealing,
One day will flash and send you crashing through the ceiling.
Thank heaven for little girls!
Thank heaven for them all, no matter where, no matter who.
Without them, what would little boys do?
Thank heaven, thank heaven, thank heaven for little girls!
Those little eyes so helpless and appealing,
One day will flash and send you crashing through the ceiling.
Thank heaven for little girls!
Thank heaven for them all, no matter where, no matter who.
Without them, what would little boys do?
Thank heaven, thank heaven, thank heaven for little girls!

IT'S A BORE

Honoré: Look at all the captivating, fascinating things there are to do!

Gaston: *(Spoken) Name two.*

Honoré: Look at all the pleasures, all the myriad of treasures we have got.

Gaston: *(Spoken) Like what?*

Honoré: Look at Paris in the spring, when each solitary thing
is more beautiful than ever before.
You can hear ev'ry tree almost saying, "Look at me!"

Gaston: *(Spoken) What color are the trees?*

Honoré: *(Spoken) Green.*

Gaston: *(Spoken) What color were they last year?*

Honoré: *(Spoken) Green.*

Gaston: *(Spoken) And next year?*

Honoré: *(Spoken) Green.*

Gaston: It's a bore.

Honoré: Don't you marvel at the pow'r of the mighty Eiffel Tow'r,
knowing there it will remain evermore?
Climbing up to the sky over ninety stories high.

Gaston: *(Spoken) How many stories?*

Honoré: *(Spoken) Ninety.*

Gaston: *(Spoken) How many yesterday?*

Honoré: *(Spoken) Ninety.*

Gaston: *(Spoken) And tomorrow?*

Honoré: *(Spoken) Ninety.*

Gaston: It's a bore.

Honoré: The river Seine!

Gaston: All it can do is flow.

Honoré: But think of wine!

Gaston: It's red or white.

Honoré: But think of girls!

Gaston: It's either yes or no, and if it's no or if it's yes, it simply couldn't matter less.

Honoré: But think of a race with your horse in seventh place,
then he suddenly begins and he catches up and wins with a roar!

Gaston: It's a bore.

Honoré: *(Spoken) Don't you dream, for heaven's sake?*

Gaston: *(Spoken) Dreaming bores me wide awake!*

Honoré: *(Spoken) Life's a gay, romantic fling!*

Gaston: *(Spoken) If you like that sort of thing!*

Honoré: *(Spoken) It's intriguing!*

Gaston: *(Spoken) It's fatiguing!*

Honoré: *(Spoken) It's a game!*

Gaston: It's the same dull world wherever you go, whatever place you are at.
The earth is round, but ev'rything on it is flat!

Honoré: Don't tell me Venice has no lure?

Gaston: Just a town without a sew'r.

Honoré: The Leaning Tower I adore.

Gaston: Indecision is a bore!

Honoré: But think of patè, then a fresh turbot grillè,
then rognons en brochette; salad, cheese, crêpes suzette!
What a thrill!

Gaston: I'd be ill!

Honoré: *(Spoken) The Mona Lisa's form and grace…*

Gaston: *(Spoken) Just another pretty face.*

Honoré: *(Spoken) Watching wintertime unfold!*

Gaston: *(Spoken) Winter really leaves me cold.*

Honoré: *(Spoken) But the dawn!*

Gaston: *(Spoken) It's a yawn! Life is blah!*

Honoré: *(Spoken) Not to moi.*

Gaston: *(Spoken) Dull as tea.*

Honoré: *(Spoken) Not to me. Just to you…*

Both: It's a bore.

THE EARTH AND OTHER MINOR THINGS

Gigi: I know about the earth and other minor things,
Why caterpillars smile and summertime has wings;
How if somewhere there's always a dawn,
The earth must be worth being on.
But there's one thing that makes a continual riddle of it:
Why, oh why I'm here in the middle of it all?
I don't belong where the crowds are.
Why don't I go where the clouds are?
I know about the leaves that fall and then are gone,
How small a kite becomes with no one holding on;
And I can't be a cloud in a storm with nowhere to go to be warm;
And as long as I can't find a clue to the riddle of it,
What am I to do in the middle of it all?
I don't belong where the crowds are.
I don't belong where the clouds are.
Then where do I belong?

PARIS IS PARIS AGAIN

Verse 1:
Honoré: Night in the sky,
From the street comes the cry
Of the rooster in search of the hen,
And Paris is Paris again.

Stars on their beat
Looking down on the sweet
Intertwining of women and men,
And Paris is Paris again.

Lovers in closets and shoes in the drawer,
Screams on the Rue Madeleine;
Swords in the park! A shot in the dark!
And Paris is spicily vicely Paris again.

Verse 2:
Moon burning bright,
And like bats in the night
Come the well-feathered demimondaine,
And Paris is Paris again.

Ladies you know,
Arm in arm with their low
Classanovas meander the Seine,
And Paris is Paris again.

Meetings at nine that tomorrow will be
Meetings with lawyers at ten;
Handfuls of hair! A tooth on the chair!
And Paris is gaudily bawdily Paris again.

SHE IS NOT THINKING OF ME

Verse 1:
Gaston: She's so gay tonight! She's like spring tonight!
She's a rollicking, frolicking thing tonight!
So disarming, soft and charming;
She is not thinking of me!
No, she's not thinking of me!

Verse 2:
In her eyes tonight, there's a glow tonight!
They're so bright, they could light Fontainebleau tonight!
She's so gracious, so vivacious;
She is not thinking of me!

Bless her little heart, crooked to the core, acting out her part.
What a rollicking, frolicking bore!
She's such fun tonight! She's a treat tonight!
You could spread her on bread, she's so sweet tonight.

So devoted, sugar-coated, that it's heartwarming to see.
Oh, she's simmering with love!
Oh, she's simmering with love!
Oh, she's not thinking of me!
She is not thinking of me!
She is not thinking of me!

Is it that painter from Brussels?
Is it that Count with the muscles?
Is it that goat with the gout?
That odious, ice-skating lout!
Is it Jacques? Or Leon?
Oh, she's hot, but it's not for Gaston!

She's a gem tonight! She's a beaut tonight!
So annoyingly, cloyingly cute tonight;
So caressing, so depressing;
She is not thinking of me!

She's so gay tonight! Oh, so gay tonight!
A gigantic, romantic cliché tonight.
How she blushes! How she gushes! How she fills me with ennui!
She's so ooh la-la-la-la!
So untrue la-la-la-la!
She is not, oh, she's not, oh, she's not, oh, she's not, no, she's not,
she is not thinking of me!

THE NIGHT THEY INVENTED CHAMPAGNE

Gigi: What time tomorrow will we get there? Can I watch you play roulette there?
May I stay up late for supper? Is it awf'lly, awf'lly upper?

Mamita: Gigi! You'll drive us wild. Stop, you silly child.

Gigi: Is ev'rybody celebrated, full of sin and dissipated?
Is it hot enough to blister? Will I be your little sister?

Mamita: Gigi, you are absurd. Not another word.

Gaston: Let her gush and jabber. Let her be enthused.
I cannot remember when I have been more amused.

Gigi: The night they invented champagne, it's plain as it can be.
They thought of you and me!
The night they invented champagne,
They absolutely knew that all we'd want to do is fly to the sky on champagne,
And shout to ev'ryone in sight, that since the world began,
No woman or a man has ever been as happy as we are tonight!

Gaston: The night they invented champagne, it's plain as it could be.
They thought of you and me!
The night they invented champagne,
They absolutely knew that all we'd want to do is fly to the sky on champagne,
And shout to ev'ryone in sight, that since the world began,
No woman or a man has ever been as happy as we are tonight!

I REMEMBER IT WELL

Honoré: We met at nine.

Mamita: We met at eight.

Honoré: I was on time.

Mamita: No, you were late.

Honoré: Ah yes! I remember it well. We dined with friends.

Mamita: We dined alone.

Honoré: A tenor sang.

Mamita: A baritone.

Honoré: Ah yes! I remember it well. That dazzling April moon!

Mamita: There was none that night, and the month was June.

Honoré: That's right! That's right!

Mamita: It warms my heart to know that you remember still the way you do.

Honoré: Ah yes! I remember it well. How often I've thought of that Friday...

Mamita: Monday

Honoré: ...night, when we had our last rendezvous. And somehow I've foolishly wondered if you might by some chance be thinking of it too? That carriage ride.

Mamita: You walked me home.

Honoré: You lost a glove.

Mamita: I lost a comb.

Honoré: Ah yes! I remember it well. That brilliant sky.

Mamita: We had some rain.

Honoré: Those Russian songs.

Mamita: From sunny Spain.

Honoré: Ah yes! I remember it well. You wore a gown of gold.

Mamita: I was all in blue.

Honoré: Am I getting old?

Mamita: Oh no! Not you! How strong you were, how young and gay; A prince of love in ev'ry way.

Honoré: Ah yes! I remember it well.

GIGI

Gaston: There's sweeter music when she speaks, isn't there?
A diff'rent bloom about her cheeks, isn't there?
Could I be wrong? Could it be so?
Oh where, oh where did Gigi go?

Gigi, am I a fool without a mind or have I merely been to blind to realize?
Oh, Gigi, why you've been growing up before my eyes!
Gigi, you're not at all the funny, awkward little girl I knew, oh no!
Over night there's been a breathless change in you.

Oh, Gigi, while you were trembling on the brink,
Was I out yonder somewhere blinking at a star?
Oh, Gigi, have I been standing up too close, or back too far?
When did your sparkle turn to fire and your warmth become desire?
Oh, what miracle has made you the way you are?

Gigi, am I a fool without a mind or have I merely been to blind to realize?
Oh, Gigi, why you've been growing up before my eyes!
Gigi, you're not at all the funny, awkward little girl I knew, oh no!
I was mad not to have seen the change in you.

Oh, Gigi, while you were trembling on the brink,
Was I out yonder somewhere blinking at a star?
Oh, Gigi, have I been standing up too close, or back too far?
When did your sparkle turn to fire and your warmth become desire?
Oh, what miracle has made you the way you are?

I'M GLAD I'M NOT YOUNG ANYMORE

Honoré: Poor boy, poor boy, downhearted and depressed and in a spin.
Poor boy, poor boy. Oh, youth can really do a fellow in.

Verse 1:
How lovely to sit here in the shade with none of the woes of man and maid;
I'm glad I'm not young anymore.
The rivals that don't exist at all; the feeling you're only two feet tall;
I'm glad that I'm not young anymore.

No more confusion, no morning-after surprise,
No self-delusion that when you're telling those lies, she isn't wise.

And even if love comes through the door; the kind that goes on forevermore;
Forevermore is shorter than before.
Oh, I'm so glad that I'm not young anymore.

Verse 2:
The tiny remark that tortures you, the fear that your friends won't like her too;
I'm glad I'm not young anymore.
The longing to end a stale affair, until you find out she doesn't care;
I'm glad that I'm not young anymore.

No more frustration, no star-crossed lover am I.
No aggravation, just one reluctant reply,
"Lady, goodbye."

The fountain of youth is dull as paint,
Methuselah is my patron saint.
I've never been so comfortable before.
Oh, I'm so glad that I'm not young anymore.

IN THIS WIDE, WIDE WORLD

Gigi: I've been hoping you'd call.
Yes, I called you.
I've been thinking, that's all I've been doing today.
Am I sorry?
I'm sorry you wounded me so.
No, please, not again, don't try to explain.
What matters to me is you forced me to see something buried inside
I can no longer hide.

In this wide, wide world, must be oh, so many girls better for you than I.
In this wide, wide world, there is someone who is more ideal for you;
Someone who's more your world:
Wiser arms, a far more knowing smile;
Charm galore she'll have,
Much more she'll have than I possess;
With so much more finesse and style.
Someone used to this wide, wide world,
Who can love and still not hope too high;
Who can live your life and give your life the things I can't supply!

And if you find her, I'll die!
So I called you today, called you to say,
After reflecting and pond'ring and thinking about you,
I would rather be mis'rable with you than without you.

SAINT-SUBBER
presents
The Los Angeles and San Francisco Light Opera Production of

Loewe and Lerner's

GiGi

A New Musical for Broadway
based on the novel by Colette

Music by | Book and Lyrics by
FREDERICK | ALAN JAY
LOEWE | LERNER

Produced by **EDWIN LESTER** and **SAINT-SUBBER**

Scenic Production Designed by **OLIVER SMITH**

Costumes Designed by **OLIVER MESSEL**

Lighting by **THOMAS SKELTON**

Orchestrations by **IRWIN KOSTAL**   Dance Arrangements by **TRUDE RITTMANN**

Musical Direction by **ROSS REIMUELLER**

Dances and Musical Numbers Staged by
ONNA WHITE

Directed by
JOSEPH HARDY